Anger
Management

The School of Emotional Literacy Series

Anger Management

Programme

Elizabeth Morris

Incentive Publishing

Acknowledgements

Grateful thanks go the editor, Eve Wilson, for her unstinting efforts and practical help in making this programme as user friendly as it is. Her experience has been invaluable. Thanks also to Rachel Carter for her help with the production of this manual.

Published in 2002 by Incentive Publishing,
Unit 6, Fernfield Farm, Whaddon Rd,
Little Horwood, Milton Keynes MK17 0PS
Website: www.incentiveplus.co.uk

British Library Cataloguing in Publication Data
A catalogue record for this book is available
from the British Library

ISBN 1-904407-00-5

Contents

The Author

Elizabeth Morris is Principal of the School of Emotional Literacy in Gloucestershire, UK. She is a psychologist, counsellor and trainer. Elizabeth also established the online Self-Esteem Advisory Service in 1999 in response to the increasing demand for information on this topic. She has developed a Post-Graduate Certificate in Emotional Literacy Development for any professional working with young people or families. The University of Bristol is currently running her programmes on Emotional Intelligence and Self-Motivation, Emotional Coaching, Self-Esteem Building and the Certificate in Emotional Competency.

Elizabeth writes extensively on the subjects of emotional literacy and self-esteem, and their application at home and school. She is frequently interviewed on radio and in the press about her emotional literacy programmes and self-esteem building.

The Editor

Eve Wilson MA, BEd (Hons), Cert Ed has spent 30 years in education, including 10 years as a Primary head teacher. She is a qualified OfSTED inspector and was an accredited trainer for NPQH during its inaugural year. Eve currently works as an educational adviser for Incentive Plus. She also edits and co-writes teachers' resources and writes her own children's stories and songs.

Introduction

Anger Management has become the most requested topic in the series of workshops run by the School of Emotional Literacy. It is closely followed by Behaviour Management, under which, of course, anger management falls. So it is obvious that youth leaders, teachers, parents – and the students who are experiencing these emotional hijacks – are all struggling to find ways to cope.

The main focus of this manual is Emotional Literacy so that is the body of information to which we turn for help.

To remind you, Emotional Literacy is the practice of

- being aware
- understanding
- appropriately expressing
- handling emotional states in ourselves and other people.

We are all born with an ability and potential in these areas, and this is our Emotional Intelligence. What we do with this ability and how we use it is our Emotional Literacy. In other words, it is how we 'read' and make sense of the emotional signals and information within ourselves, and those sent from other people.

Emotional Literacy involves using both skills and attitudes.

The **skills** include:

- self-awareness
- self-management (through, for example, stress management techniques)
- impulse control
- active listening
- empathy
- the ability to understand non-verbal cues
- conflict resolution
- mediation

The **attitudes** involve:

- having an optimistic outlook
- placing equal importance on emotional and cognitive matters
- having focus
- having an acceptance of other people and how they are

The skills can be taught through training and practising. The attitudes can be developed through, for instance, using a facilitative and co-operative teaching style or style of leadership. These two aspects combine and help students to develop into well-balanced and emotionally maturing individuals. With increasing emotional maturity, students become more capable of stronger academic achievement since they are not psychologically involved with inner tensions and emotional turmoil. They can form better relationships with adults and peers, make friends and protect themselves from bullies. They are also likely to be healthier since our immune systems tend to become depleted when we have unacknowledged and unprocessed anxiety building up inside. Obviously, understanding Emotional Literacy development can help by giving us an insight into ways in which to manage our feelings, and in particular our anger outbursts.

Emotional Hijacks

The first way that looking at Emotional Literacy development can help is by providing an explanation for the phenomenon of an angry outburst. Daniel Goleman called these 'Emotional Hijacks' in his book, *Emotional Intelligence: why it can matter more than IQ*. He was referring to the physiological flooding of the cognitive centres in the brain that happen when we become angry or fearful. Our endocrine system sends bio-chemicals into our bloodstream to prepare us for 'flight or fight' and these begin to disable our ability to think and plan.   At that point we have moved into survival mode and our whole bodies are primed to act first, think later.   There is now evidence that the neural links between the emotional sites in the brain and the cognitive sites work faster and are far greater in number than those from the cognitive to the emotional.   It therefore takes much longer for the thinking systems in the brain to send back the information that this situation is not a survival issue and that a more measured approach would be better. It is therefore not surprising that we have all experienced emotional hijacks at some time or other!

Developing self-awareness

The second way that Emotional Literacy development can help is by demonstrating the importance of self-awareness as a skill. Without this self-awareness it is impossible to manage our behaviour and actions well. For example, unless we are aware that we are feeling anxious we cannot decide what to do to help ourselves. We may be feeling apprehensive about an exam we have to take. If we are aware that we are feeling anxious, there are many things we can do to help ourselves. We can decide to:

- talk to a friend about it
- ask for extra help revising
- do some more reading about a topic of which we are unsure
- take a walk to calm ourselves down before starting to study again
- make sure we eat food that will help us learn more effectively
- have enough rest before the exam

There are various exercises in Emotional Literacy material that can help to focus individuals on their own thoughts, feelings and ideas. These are important to incorporate into the curriculum but it is probably even more important to integrate a self-reflective period into any activity you are doing: this encourages students to develop the habit of noticing how they have been reacting to the material you have presented.

Stages

The third way Emotional Literacy can help is by emphasising that there are three different stages to Anger Management and that, because of the physiology involved, these need to be tackled separately.

The stages are:

- pre-emotional hijack
- hijack
- post-emotional hijack

Pre-emotional hijack

In the pre-emotional hijack stage the bio-chemicals such as adrenalin are only just beginning to kick in. There is still some 'wriggle room', where a person can STOP, THINK and then DECIDE to do something different. This might include using some stress management techniques to calm down, such as counting to ten. It may be to listen carefully to the signals coming from your body so that you know what help you need in order to manage the angry response more effectively. At this stage self-awareness is critical because this is what enables the person to understand what their body is saying to them. If they pick these messages up they will be able to buy themselves time to keep the 'biochemical soup' in their brains from becoming too concentrated. At this point they can use techniques such as asking someone else for help, visualising, humour and other methods that help break the cycle.

A complication at this stage is that some of the other strategies that they will have been using to try to deal with their difficult emotions will be coming under strain. For example, the following are all ways people have developed to try to escape from their uncomfortable feelings:

- denial of particular feelings
- acting-out behaviour which provokes responses in other people and creates so much furore that the original emotional stimulus can be ignored
- oppositional defiance (which is a trademark of some young people who find a way to deal with their feelings of impotence and uncertainty by opposing everything you say, do or stand for)

These are not very effective strategies, although in the absence of concrete positive emotional competencies they are better than nothing.

What happens when something triggers off the beginnings of an emotional hijack is that all those other denied, or acted-out, feelings come to the fore. They are like accelerants in a fire, enflaming the feeling that is emerging in reaction to the situation, and so making the size of the emotional hijack very much greater than the situation seems to call for.

Teaching emotional competency as a standard part of the day will gradually help students to develop new ways to cope with the multitude of feelings they experience and, after a while, make the pre-emotional hijack stage far less fraught. It will similarly help young people who may have a history of over-reaction or of violent temper outbursts.

Hijack

When a hijack occurs, the brain floods with chemicals and all rational thought becomes impossible. This is the 'Danger Time' when action is taken which may well be regretted later on.

Post-emotional hijack

In the post-emotional hijack stage, when the brain has become flooded with emotional charges, it is important to take at least 20 minutes to calm down before starting on any negotiation, reparation or other conflict management techniques. At this point the important skills for people who are trying to help are active listening and empathy.

Teacher/Facilitator's Emotional Literacy

One last point to make about Anger Management and Emotional Literacy is that a lot of the success of teaching it to young people lies in you and your own Emotional Literacy. Students certainly learn best by osmosis! An area to explore in yourself is your own reaction to anger and conflict. These are things that many of us feel very uncomfortable to be around. Supporting yourself by being aware of, understanding, expressing and learning how to handle your own emotional responses can make a great difference to the learning and emotional development of your students.

Teaching young people the basic tools of Emotional Literacy and, within that, giving them equipment to manage their anger effectively can have many positive effects on their daily environment.

Students:

- are able to recognise and understand feelings; to handle and express them well
- become less stressed
- are better listeners and more empathic with one another
- have improved concentration as their attention span increases
- develop better self-control and reduced impulsivity
- form deeper relationships and keep them longer
- develop better problem-solving abilities
- are less violent
- have the potential to be high quality parents

(Adapted from Sharp 2001, *Nurturing Emotional Literacy*)

If you are struggling to work your way through an anger management programme with a student try the following tips:

- Use a video to see what could be changed
- Watch it together when both of you are calm
- Reward yourself regularly for giving this your best shot
- Use all the support you can get

Suggested Ways in Which to Use the Session Plans

This pack of plans follows the steps of the pre-hijack, emotional hijack and post-hijack stages outlined in the introduction. It offers a variety of exercises that can be used to form a complete anger management programme. It is possible to use some of the exercises as a 'one-off session': that depends on how knowledgeable and sophisticated the students are about social and emotional learning.

Each session is based on a one-hour slot. However, all the activities may be shortened or extended as dictated by the group and the teacher. Approximate timings are given as a guide only and will vary according to the skills, knowledge and particular needs of each group of students. Allow an activity more time if it is going particularly well. Remember, a great deal of learning takes place through incidental discussion!

Each session consists of the same basic layout, giving the aims, resources needed and a detailed outline of the method. Photocopiable Student Sheets are included with each session. Where it is felt the teacher may need more information, this is included as a Teacher Sheet.

Have fun!

Assessment

Assessment is recognised as being crucial to effective teaching and learning. Each of these sessions includes numerous opportunities for staff observation and assessment of the individual student's work. The worksheets themselves will form part of this continuous assessment procedure. It is hoped that this will be formative assessment that will then be used to 'pace' the lessons more effectively to the students' skills, knowledge and abilities.

Methods of assessment that could be used include:

Teacher   Observation of group interaction
                   Analysis of worksheets

Other staff   Observation of incidents when students use
                   techniques learned during other times of the day.

Student   Self-Assessment: Learning Logs – a sample log
                   which may be photocopied and used by the
                   individual students is supplied. (Student Sheet
                   1:4) It is suggested that students review their
                   learning at the end of every session. They could
                   also be encouraged to record incidents when
                   they use the techniques learned and to ask staff
                   to comment on these. However, do stress the
                   importance of making positive comments!

Session 1
Feelings Focus

Aims:

To realise there are many different words to describe different feelings.

To demonstrate an understanding of new 'feeling' words.

Resources:

Student Sheet 1:1 Mind Mapping of Feeling

Teacher Sheet 1:1 Mind Mapping of Feeling

Student Sheet 1:2 Word List of Emotions

Student Sheet 1:3 The Six Basic Feelings

Student Sheet 1:4 Learning Log

Teacher Sheet 1:2 Ideas for Using the Learning Log

Method:

Announce that the topic for the next few lessons is going to be 'Feelings'. Today you are going to start off by finding out how many words there are to describe our feelings. Start off with a whole group 'ideas-shower' and cover the board with as many feeling words as you can all come up with.

(Allow 5 minutes)

Ask the students to sit in pairs.

Each pair should then choose one word and talk about a situation when they felt like that. If anyone is reluctant or feels threatened, ask them to imagine a situation that might make someone else feel like that.

(Allow 10 minutes)

Give out Student Sheet 1:1.

Explain that there are many words to describe each emotion, and then ask each pair to write their chosen feeling word in the centre of the sheet.

Working together, they are now to add 10 associated words to the 'Mind Map'. You can start them off by putting the example on Teacher Sheet 1:1 up on the board.

(Allow 10 minutes)

Hand out Student Sheet 1:2.

Ask students to read through the list of emotions.

When they have had a few moments ask them to volunteer any unfamiliar words. If necessary, start them off by choosing a fairly easy word yourself; make it one that someone is likely to know the meaning of. With each word that is called out take time to discuss its meaning with the students.

Now ask students to tick off any words they have used in their Mind Map. Go round the whole group asking for new words, which they have used, and which are not on the list. Ask the other students to add these extra words to their lists.

(Allow 15 minutes)

Explain that there are six basic feelings:

- anger
- sadness
- happiness
- fear
- surprise
- disgust

Tell the group that the feeling words they have put on the board will be:

- synonyms for one another, or
- 'gradations' of a basic feeling, or
- combinations of these six feelings.

Here are some examples to give them:

Synonym: sad/unhappy, startled/surprised

Gradation: grief-stricken/unhappy, furious/cross

Combination: shame = fear and disgust

Hand out Student Sheet 1:3.

Ask for suggestions from the whole group for one word from the list to go into each box. Tell the students to write each word in an appropriate place on the sheet. Now, still working in pairs, ask students to write four other words in each section.

(Allow 10 minutes)

Ask each pair to join another pair to exchange ideas. Add any new words from the others in the group of four.

(Allow 5 minutes)

Bring students back into a whole group.

Ask for any unfamiliar words that students have learned. Allow discussion for each of these.

Tell students to keep the word lists safely for later use.

(5 minutes)

Finally, give each student a Learning Log (Student Sheet 1:4) and explain how to use these.

If time allows, play a class game of charades, with individuals miming an emotion. If necessary, the game could be played in smaller groups if the students find the whole group too threatening.

(Rest of session)

Mind Mapping of Feeling

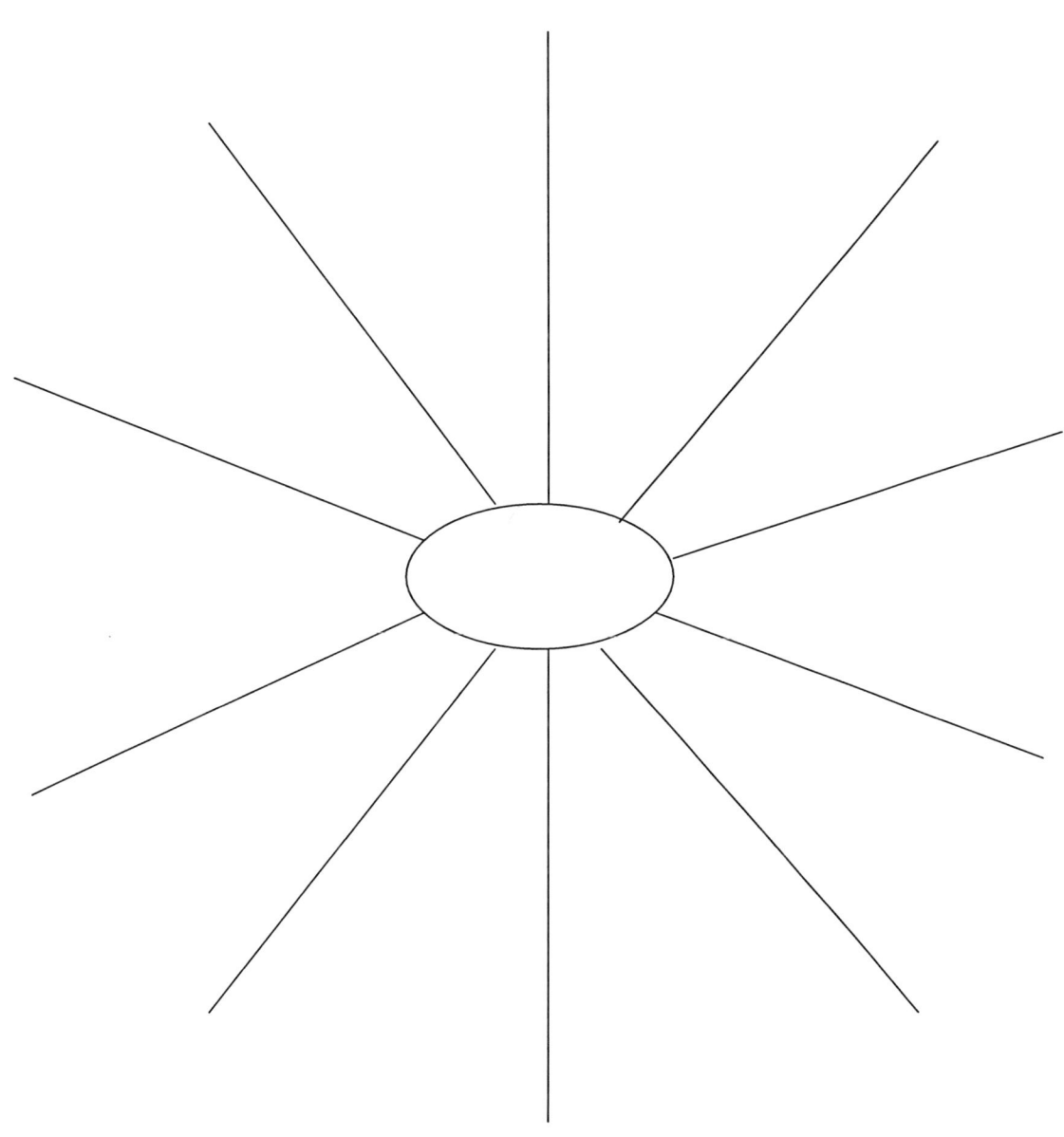

Mind Mapping of Feeling

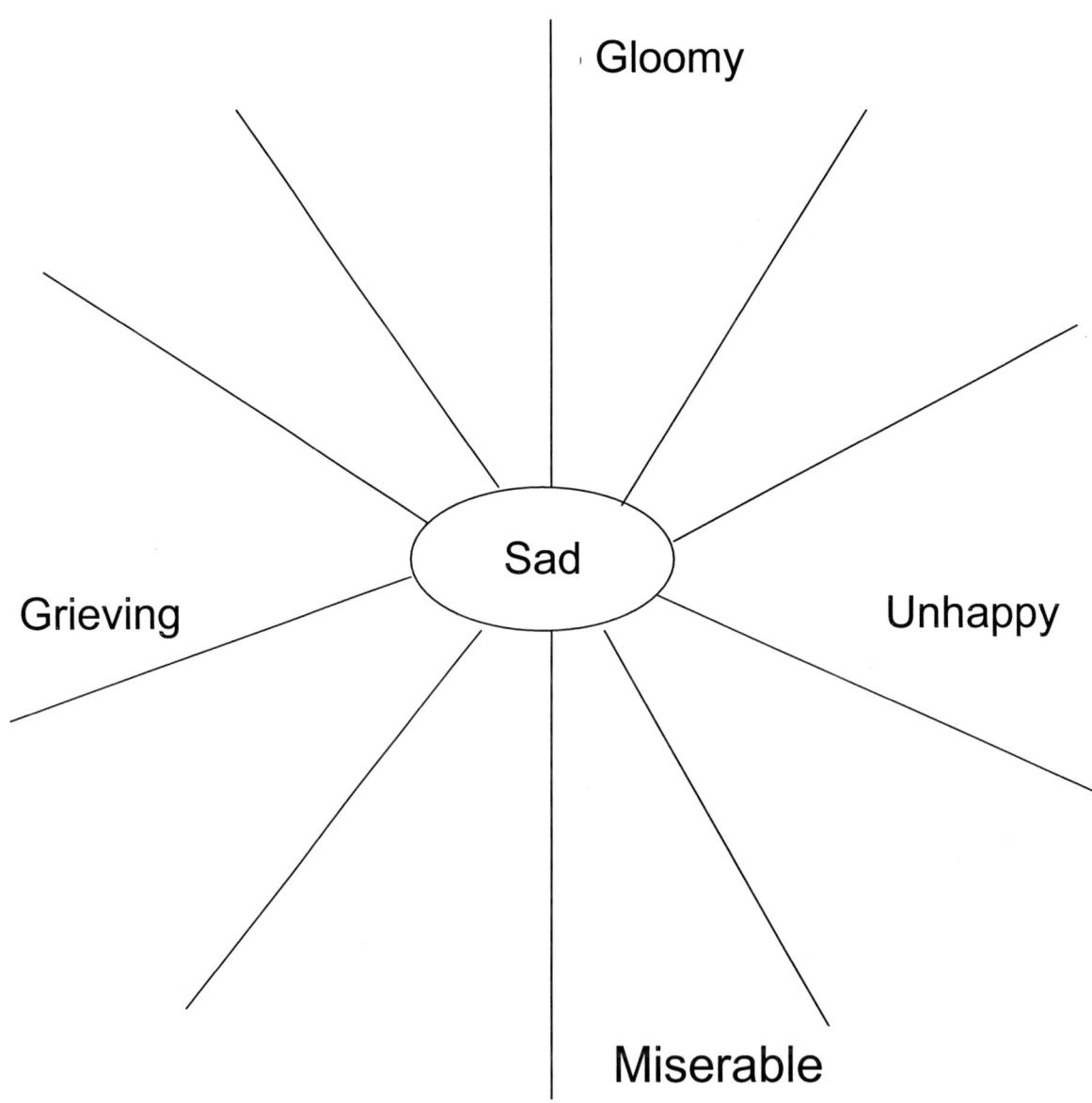

Gloomy

Grieving

Sad

Unhappy

Miserable

Word List of Emotions

Emotion (a - b)	Emotion (c - d)	Emotion (e - g)	Emotion (h - k)	Emotion (l - o)	Emotion (p - r)	Emotion (s - t)	Emotion (u - z)
Abandoned	Caddish	Eager	Happy	Lackadaisical	Pain	Sad	Unctuous
Absent	Cagey	Easy going	Hassled	Languid	Panicked	Safe	Undervalued
Abused	Callous	Ecstatic	Hateful	Lazy	Paranoid	Sanctimonious	Uneasy
Accepted	Calm	Effervescent	Helpful	Left out	Passionate	Sapped	Unprotected
Acclaimed	Cantankerous	Elated	Helpless	Lethargic	Pathetic	Satisfied	Unsafe
Accused	Care free	Electrified	High	Likeable	Peaceful	Scared	Unsociable
Acquiescent	Chided	Embarrassed	Hollow	Logical	Peeved	Screwed up	Unwanted
Adamant	Churlish	Empty	Homesick	Lonely	Persecuted	Self-confident	Uprooted
Adequate	Clever	Enchanted	Honoured	Loser, like a	Petrified	Selfish	Upset
Adoring	Comfortable	Energetic	Hopeful	Lousy	Pissed off	Sensitive	Uptight
Affable	Compliant	Enthusiastic	Hopeless	Lovable	Playful	Settled	Used
Affectionate	Concerned	Envious	Horrible	Loving	Pleasant	Sexy	Useless
Affirmed	Confident	Evasive	Hostile	Low	Possessive	Shallow	
Afraid	Conned	Exasperated	Humble	Loyal	Powerful	Shame	Vain
Agonised	Cornered	Excited	Hurt	Lustful	Powerless	Shocked	Valued
Alarmed	Cowardly	Exhausted	Hyper		Preoccupied	Shy	Vicious
Alienated	Cranky	Exhilarated	Hysterical	Mad	Pressured	Silly	Violent
Aloof	Creative	Explosive		Manic	Pushy	Sluggish	Vivacious
Ambivalent	Cruel	Exultant	Idiotic	Manipulated	Put out	Sorry	Vulnerable
Angry	Curious		Ignored	Maternal	Puzzled	Spiritual	
Annoyed	Cut off	Fabulous	Immobilised	Mawkish		Squashed	Wanted
Anxious	Cynical	False	Impatient	Merry	Quarrelsome	Strained	Warped
Apathetic		Fantastic	Imposed	Miserable	Queasy	Stumped	Weak
Appreciated	Daring	Fatigued	upon	Misunderstood	Quiet	Stunned	Wicked
Astounded	Daunted	Fawning	Impressed	Mixed up	Quivery	Stupid	Wilful
Attractive	Deceitful	Fearful	Impulsive	Motivated		Sulky	Wishy-
Avaricious	Defeated	Flustered	Inadequate	Mystified	Rational	Sullen	washy
Averse	Dejected	Foolish	Inattentive		Ravenous	Sure	Wonderful
Awed	Delighted	Frantic	Incompetent	Nasty	Reborn	Surprised	Worried
Awkward	Dependent	Free	Independent	Needy	Reckless	Suspicious	Worthless
	Depressed	Fresh	Indignant	Negative	Refreshed		Worthy
Bad	Deprived	Fretful	Infatuated	Nervous	Rejected	Taunted	Wronged
Balmy	Desperate	Friendless	Inferior	Nettled	Relaxed	Teased	
Barmy	Destructive	Friendly	Infuriated	Nice	Relieved	Tempted	Zany
Beaten	Determined	Frightened	Inhibited	Nostalgic	Remorseful	Tense	Zealous
Beautiful	Different	Frigid	Insecure	Numb	Repulsive	Threatened	
Betrayed	Diffident	Frivolous	Insincere		Reserved	Thrilled	
Bewildered	Diminished	Frustrated	Inspired	Oblivious	Restless	Thwarted	
Bitter	Dirty	Full	Intimidated	Obsessed	Restrained	Tired	
Blasé	Disappointed	Funny	Intrepid	Odd	Revengeful	Torn	
Blissful	Discontented		Involved	Offended	Revolted	Touched	
Bold	Dismayed	Generous	Invulnerable	Opposed	Romantic	Touchy	
Bombastic	Dissatisfied	Gentle	Isolated	Optimistic	Rueful	Trapped	
Bored	Distracted	Glad		Outraged		Truculent	
Brave	Distraught	Glowing	Jaded	Overlooked		Turned off	
Burdened	Disturbed	Good	Jealous	Overwhelmed			
Burned out	Divided	Gorgeous	Jinxed	Owed			
	Dominated	Grateful	Joyous				
	Dubious	Greedy	Jubilant				
	Dull	Grieving	Judgemental				
	Dumb	Guilty	Jumpy				
		Gullible					
		Gutless	Keen				
		Gutted	Kind				

The Six Basic Feelings

Anger	Sadness	Happiness

Fear	Surprise	Disgust

Learning Log

Name

My Own Set of Rules

Times when I've used the things I've learned

What I learned in Session 1

....

What I learned in Session 2

....

What I learned in Session 3

....

What I learned in Session 4

....

What I learned in Session 5

....

What I learned in Session 6

....

What I learned in Session 7

....

What I learned in Session 8

....

What I learned in Session 9

....

What I learned in Session 10

....

Ideas for Using the Learning Log

It is suggested that the students are given their individual Learning Log at the end of Session 1.

Stress that this is for their personal use and that it does not have to be shown to anyone else unless they wish to do so. This is a unique, personal record of their learning during the Anger Management Programme. Ask them to write up their thoughts and feelings as they go through the Programme, but encourage them to be positive!

They may use the back page of the Log to make their own comments on incidents that they feel they handled well or they may ask involved staff or other adults to make positive comments for them.

Session 2
Different Kinds of Anger

Aims:

To identify a variety of words that describe anger.

To place these on an Anger Continuum and recognise the different levels of intensity.

To begin to understand the idea of an Emotional Hijack.

Resources:

Student Sheet 2:1 Continuum for Anger Words

Teacher Sheet 2:1 What is an Emotional Hijack?

Paper plates

Sellotape

Lollipop sticks to stick on to back of plates to make grips for masks

Scissors

Board

Crayons, felt-tipped pens, etc

Method:

Tell the students that you are going to do the next 'feelings session' on Anger Management. In this session they will be making masks to show the range of different faces we wear when we are angry. They will also be learning about something called an Emotional Hijack.

Ask the students to 'ideas-shower' a range of words that describe someone who is angry and write them up on the board. You can refer them back to their 'feelings' word lists made during the previous session. Find as many words as possible.

(Allow 10 minutes)

Once you have a full board of 'anger' words, ask the students to form smaller groups of four and arrange the words in a continuum (Student Sheet 2:1). Explain that the adjectives must be placed from mild and minor on the left to severe, major and intense on the right. If it helps, start them off with the two ends of the continuum, either by choosing the words yourself or by asking them to call out the words they think describe the most angry feeling and the word for the least angry.

(Allow 5 minutes)

Once this is completed, ask a volunteer from each group to call out their list. There is no absolutely correct way to do the continuum, some words will be level with one another in intensity and others open to some individual variation. The main point is that they recognise that there are different levels of intensity.

Ask the students to pair up and distribute the mask-making materials. Tell them that they have to choose a feeling word from the continuum and make a mask showing a face that represents that emotion.

Exaggerate the features so that the feeling comes across very clearly. You can show an example of this if you have already made a mask yourself.

(Allow 15 minutes)

Once this is done ask the students to join up with another pair.   In turn each pair holds up their mask and tells a story of a time when they felt like this. Each person in the pair takes a turn with their mask.

(Allow 10 minutes)

Finish with a whole group discussion on what happens when people get very angry. They will be right at the top of the continuum and have an 'Emotional Hijack' where they find it hard to think well and feel flooded with their angry feelings, (see Teacher Sheet 2:1). Ask the group questions such as:

- How do other people feel when they are around someone who is having an Angry Emotional Hijack?
- How do they think the angry person feels in addition to being angry?
- Will any other emotions be involved too?
- How long does a hijack last?

(Rest of session)

Student Sheet 2:1 *Continuum for Anger Words*

What is an 'Emotional Hijack'?

When people get very angry, they are right at the top of the feeling continuum and their bloodstream is flooded with 'fight or flight' bio-chemicals, such as adrenalin.

These bio-chemicals are sent into the bloodstream by the adrenal glands because our bodies prepare themselves to deal with situations where we think we are in danger. Our bodies are very good at dealing with these situations – the only problem being that we keep thinking that we are in the middle of one of these emergencies, even when we aren't!

We do this because, right back at the beginning of our evolution into becoming the human beings we are today, we had to live a dangerous life out hunting and surviving in wild conditions. In those times our only advantage might have been our ability to fight back fiercely when we were attacked. Now, of course, our world is not like that, but our bodies have not quite caught up with the fact.

In emotional situations when we are right at the top of the continuum, we are experiencing an emotional hijack. This is when our blood chemicals are telling us to act, and that message is so strong that our neo-cortex (the top part of the brain where we do most of our logical thinking), cannot operate properly (recall a time when you could hardly think because a siren was sounding near you). In an emotional hijack the person is flooded with feeling and can't think effectively; they are taken over by the emotion they are experiencing.

Session 3
What I Get Angry About

Aims:

To be able to identify which situations, people or physiological conditions trigger anger.

To consider ways to handle these.

Resources:

Teacher Sheet 3:1 Points to Emphasise

Student Sheet 3:1 What I Get Angry About

Method:

Do a brief recap on the last two sessions once you have the students' attention. Remind them that the purpose of these sessions is to build up a whole range of ways they can use to manage their angry feelings. They have already seen how many different feelings human beings can feel and how many different levels of 'feeling angry' there are. Today they are going to find out what different things trigger them into feeling angry in the first place.

Ask students to work in pairs. Distribute the worksheets and ask the pairs to consider the different things that spark off angry feelings in themselves. After discussion they are individually to complete the first column 'Triggers' on Student Sheet 3:1.

(Allow 15 minutes)

When they have worked on their own list of triggers ask them to form their pair again and then join up with another pair to discuss their findings.   Ask them to notice any similarities and differences between each other's list of examples.

(Allow 10 minutes)

Once they have completed that, you can ask for a volunteer from each group to tell the rest of the students in what ways they were the same or different.   Build up an inventory of these on the board as they talk.

(5 minutes)

Next, ask them to work on their own again listing a few ways that they have found to deal with the examples they wrote down. They will fill in the second column on Student Sheet 3:1 under 'What I do'.

(Allow 10 minutes)

Finish the session with a whole group discussion about the methods they have come up with. Students can volunteer their examples and others can give their suggestions. While they are talking you can take the opportunity to write the points on the board.

Ask the students if they have ever seen anyone handle their anger very effectively:

- who?
- how did they do that?
- why did it seem to be effective?

Finish with a question to the group about what they have learnt from the session. You can put it up on the board as the 'Wow, How, Now' questions:

Wow – 'I didn't know that.' or 'I knew but had forgotten.'
How – 'Oh, that's how to do that.'
Now – 'This is what I'm going to do now/next time.'

(Rest of session)

Teacher Sheet 3:1
Points to Emphasise

Anger is just one of a wide range of human emotions.

It serves useful purposes.

It can be protective.

It can warn you of something that is not to your liking.

There are effective and ineffective ways to deal with angry feelings.

We can choose whether to respond in a constructive or non-constructive way.

No one else can 'make' us angry; we, ourselves, choose how to respond to the stimulus.

If you have time you can extend the discussion into body language and how we pick up signals from other people. You can also explore how people's bodies respond when they feel angry.

Student Sheet 3:1
What I Get Angry About

Many people react angrily to things and many people react angrily to the same things, but sometimes you can react angrily to something that is personal just to you. What are the things that you feel angry about? Who tends to trigger your anger? What situations frustrate you? Use this sheet to make notes about what you do to deal with your feelings of anger and how you express it: do you hide it? Do you try to calm down? Write a list under the right-hand column.

Triggers	What I do
Where: E.g., bus	Try to sit on my own Feel angry
Who: Joe Bloggs	Don't look at him
What: Kicks me	Tell him to stop
When: In the morning	Hope he's ill that day

Session 4
What I Can do When my Anger is Building Up

Aim:

To help students have a selection of options to use when they feel angry.

Resource:

Student Sheet 4:1 Things I do When I am Beginning to Feel Angry

Method:

Tell the students at the start that you are going to carry on with the anger management sessions. This session you will all be discussing and practising different ideas on how to deal with feelings of anger when you might be building up to an emotional hijack.   Explain that everyone will have different ways of dealing with it and the best idea is to share them all and practise them so that everybody ends up with more options that they had at the start.

Begin with things that they do generally to make themselves feel good.   'Ideas-shower' these. They could include playing sport, seeing friends, watching TV, playing video games…

(Allow 15 minutes)

Now ask the students to work in groups of four.

Ask them to discuss the ways they use to help themselves feel better when they are building up a lot of anger and tension.

Hand out Student Sheet 4:1.

Ask students to conduct a mini-survey within their small group.

(Allow 15 minutes)

Now bring the whole group together and ask for contributions on what they have discovered. Still working as a whole group, discuss the various merits of each. Explain that you will be discussing some of these in more detail in later sessions.

(10 minutes)

Ask the students to split into pairs, two from each group. Name one of the pairs 'A' and the other 'B'. Explain that 'A' is very angry because a teacher has blamed them for writing graffiti, which they haven't done. 'B' is to try to talk through the situation and calm 'A' down.

(5 minutes)

Now they are to reverse roles. This time, 'B' is angry because Mum has grounded them for an unfair reason.   'A' is to attempt to defuse 'B's anger.

(5 minutes)

Hold a general whole group discussion and encourage all students to discuss the value of peer mediation.

(Rest of session)

Student Sheet 4:1
Things I do When I am Beginning to Feel Angry

Discuss these with your friends and put a tick for every one each of you uses. Which are the most popular ideas?

Find an adult to talk to about how you are feeling. ☐

Imagine yourself in a calm place. ☐

Talk to yourself ☐

Be honest and assertive to the person who is

upsetting you and use 'I' messages. ☐

Smile! ☐

Give someone else a helping hand. ☐

Visualise/draw/write about the person you would

most like to be. ☐

Think of a hero or heroine you admire and what

they would do. ☐

Find someone to help you when you begin to struggle. ☐

Ask your friend to help (peer mediation). ☐

Sit on your hands and count to 10. ☐

Find a way to express your energy physically, perhaps

by running, jumping, or hitting a pillow. ☐

Apologise. ☐

Do some heart-centred breathing. ☐

Put on a tape or some music. ☐

………………………………………………… ☐

………………………………………………… ☐

………………………………………………… ☐

………………………………………………… ☐

Session 5
When I Talk to Myself

Aims:

To show students how to soothe and calm themselves with positive self-talk.
To understand this method of stress management.

Resources:

Student Sheet 3:1 What I Get Angry About (completed in Session 3)
Student Sheet 5:1 Don't Be Negative!
Teacher Sheet 5:1 Don't Be Negative!
Chalk/pens and board

Method:

Tell the students that you are going to be teaching them about a new way to manage their anger and stress today and that it is a very useful way because they don't need any equipment to do it. The technique you are going to be working with today is called 'self-talk'. Ask the whole group what they think this is. Ask them to suggest descriptions and give examples of self-talk, and write them up on the board. You may need to give some examples at first. For example:

"It is the words we say to ourselves inside."

"It is a conversation we have with ourselves."

"It goes on all the time."

"We talk to ourselves more than to anyone else."

"The way we talk to ourselves makes a big difference to how we feel."

(15 minutes)

Ask students to go back to Student Sheet 3:1. Taking it in turns, ask each person to read out one of their examples. These are written on the board and you can add some of your own ideas if necessary. For example:

you get an F on your report card

you meet a new person who acts rudely

(10 minutes)

Going down the statements, ask other volunteers what they might say to themselves in the situation written up. Then ask the group to decide whether that was negative or positive self-talk. They can do this as a voting system – everyone who thinks positive puts up their hands, everyone who thinks negative puts up their hands. For each negative one ask them to redefine it and find something positive to say instead.

For example, if someone says they would say "I'm rubbish at school" if they got an F on their report card, a positive thing to say instead would be "I didn't do so well on this report but I know I can do better. I am going to get a higher mark next time."

Or "My Dad will kill me when he sees this" could be changed to "I will remind Dad of the things I do well when I show him this."

(15 minutes)

Continue until you have covered all the situations/people/times. Make sure all the students take some part in this. Now give out Student Sheet 5:1 and ask students individually to work through the examples.

(10 minutes)

Finish by emphasising the value of positive self-talk and, if time allows, ask students for examples of this that they may begin to use now following this session.

(Rest of session)

Don't Be Negative!

Turn each of these negative statements into a positive one.

Negative	Positive
I'm rubbish at that	
I don't learn easily	
No one cares about me	
I wish I were someone else	
There are lots of things about myself I'd change if I could	
It takes me a long time to get used to something new	
I'm fat and ugly	
I'm no good	
I don't care what happens to me	
I can't be depended on	

Don't Be Negative!

Turn each of these negative statements into a positive one.

Negative	Positive
I'm rubbish at that	I'm learning how to do that There are many things I can do
I don't learn easily	I'm a thorough learner I learn easily another way
No one cares about me	I care about me
I wish I were someone else	I have a great imagination
There are lots of things about myself I'd change if I could	I can change the way I am if I want to
It takes me a long time to get used to something new	I like to learn all about new things
I'm fat and ugly	Compared with other people I'm slimmer and nicer looking than some, and plumper and more average looking than others
I'm no good	There are several things I'm good at, for instance …
I don't care what happens to me	I'm important
I can't be depended on	I can keep promises

Session 6
Melt Down 1!

Aim:

To elicit from students a description of how they react when they experience an emotional hijack.

Resources:

Student Sheet 6:1 What is an 'Emotional Hijack'?

Student Sheet 6:2 When I had an Emotional Hijack

Teacher Sheet 2:1 What is an 'Emotional Hijack'?

Chalk/pens and board

Felt-tipped pens, crayons, pencils, etc

Large sheets of drawing paper

The steps of anger management already written up

Method:

Tell the students that you will be doing another session on anger management together today. They will be learning more in this session and the next one about 'emotional hijacks', and what they can do when they have experienced one. Ask them if they remember this term from an earlier session and what it describes.

Explain that an emotional hijack will have physical effects on that individual. Give out Student Sheet 6:1 and allow a few minutes for students to read it and pose any questions they may have.

(Allow 10 minutes)

Now ask the students to form pairs and take turns talking to one another about a time when they think they experienced an emotional hijack, using the following prompts:

- What happened?
- What triggered it?
- How did it end?
- How did their body feel while it was happening?

Ask them to name themselves 'A' or 'B'. 'A' is to tell 'B' about their experience first and 'B' is to listen without interrupting.

(Allow 5 minutes)

Ask them to swap over so that 'B' talks to 'A' and 'A' doesn't interrupt.

(Further 5 minutes)

Once they have each had a turn they can complete Student Sheet 6:2.

(10 minutes)

Once the students have had the opportunity to record the reactions of both, hold an informal group discussion:

- What were the most common physical signs?
- Were there any unusual effects?
- Did their bodies both feel the same or were they different?

(10 minutes)

Working in pairs, using the resources provided (pens, crayons, paper etc), ask the students to produce a quick cartoon picture to illustrate an emotional hijack showing some of the physical effects. Emphasise that ability in art is not a priority and that the cartoons can be as humorous as the students like.

(Allow 10 minutes)

Finish with a quick 'exhibition' of the cartoons produced.

(Rest of session)

Student Sheet 6:1
What is an 'Emotional Hijack'?

When people get very angry, they are right at the top of the feeling continuum and their bloodstream is flooded with 'fight or flight' bio-chemicals, such as adrenalin.

These bio-chemicals are sent into the bloodstream by the adrenal glands because our bodies prepare themselves to deal with situations where we think we are in danger. Our bodies are very good at dealing with these situations – the only problem being that we keep thinking that we are in the middle of one of these emergencies, even when we aren't!

We do this because, right back at the beginning of our evolution into becoming the human beings we are today, we had to live a dangerous life out hunting and surviving in wild conditions. In those times our only advantage might have been our ability to fight back fiercely when we were attacked. Now, of course, our world is not like that, but our bodies have not quite caught up with the fact.

In emotional situations when we are right at the top of the continuum, we are experiencing an emotional hijack. This is when our blood chemicals are telling us to act, and that message is so strong that our neo-cortex (the top part of the brain where we do most of our logical thinking), cannot operate properly (recall a time when you could hardly think because a siren was sounding near you). In an emotional hijack the person is flooded with feeling and can't think effectively; they are taken over by the emotion they are experiencing.

When I Had an Emotional Hijack

What happened?	
What triggered it?	
How did it end?	
How did your body feel while it was happening?	

Session 7
Melt Down 2!

Aims:

To show students that there are opportunities to stop themselves before exploding.

To help them learn another technique for managing anger and to understand that there are three stages to deal with.

Resources:

Student Sheet 7:1 The Three Stages of an Emotional Hijack
Board and pens

Method:

Remind the students that having an emotional hijack can have detrimental physical effects: ask for some suggestions from the previous session.

Remind them that this is because of the fact that our bodies get charged up with very strong 'bio-chemicals', such as adrenalin, from our endocrine system, when we get angry.

(Allow 10 minutes)

Ask them if anyone has ever told them to count to 10? Why would they do this?

Answer: If we take a few moments these bio-chemicals have a chance to dissipate a little. These bio-chemicals add to our feeling of anger. It is as if our bodies are all prepared to fight when they are in our bloodstream.

Explain that there are three stages to an emotional hijack (write them on the board):

1. Pre-Emotional Hijack
2. HIJACK
3. Post-Emotional Hijack

It is only during the pre-hijack stage that we can easily take steps to diffuse our anger.

Lead a group discussion on when would be the best time to 'count to 10' if they are heading towards an emotional hijack.

Answer: The answer that will emerge is that there is no one right time in the pre-emotional hijack stage. In fact, it probably needs to be done several times if the first time only reduces the building anger a little.

(15 minutes)

Strongly reiterate that it is only during the building-up time that a person can count to 10 and start to calm down before they do something that will end up badly. If they get to the point of exploding, it will be then that they may hit out or say something they later regret. They run the risk of being left with a situation

54

where some damage has been done, either to a person, a room, or object, themselves, or a relationship.   This is when new techniques need to be used.

Ask the class to get into pairs. In their pairs they are to think about the HIJACK stage, when a person has exploded with anger:

- Do they need to count to 10 then too?
- Do they think that counting to 10 gives them long enough? (In fact, it takes at least 20 minutes for our bodies to return to equilibrium, so counting to 10 is only the very beginning!)
- Ask them to start thinking about what they would need if they were in the middle of an emotional hijack.

(5 minutes)

Hold a brief group discussion at this point to hear their ideas.

(5 minutes)

Give out Student Sheet 7:1.

Suggest that they all go back to the emotional hijack examples they were talking about in Session 6, choose one to describe and then fill in the worksheet.

(10 minutes)

Now form pairs again and ask them to think about what they would need in the post-emotional hijack phase:

- How could they get more time for themselves?

- What else could they do?
- How could they resolve the difficulty that their angry behaviour had created?
- What skills would they need at this point?

(5 minutes)

Ask for some volunteers to talk about their examples and lead a group discussion on ways to repair the damage after an emotional hijack. Stress the importance of having time to calm down and start thinking more clearly before this sorting out can happen.

(Rest of session)

Student Sheet 7:1
The Three Stages of an Emotional Hijack

Situation (use an example from your Student Sheet 6:1)

....

....

....

Pre-emotional Hijack:
When could I have counted to 10?

HIJACK

Post-emotional Hijack

After the Storm

Aims:

To help students to learn about empathy and be able to put themselves in another person's place.

To understand more about what happens after an emotional hijack.

Resources:

Student Sheet 8:1 Situation Story

Teacher Sheet 8:1 Situation Story

Student Sheet 8:2 Possible Reasons for Josh's Bad Mood

Teacher Sheet 8:2 Questions About the Story

Board and pens

Method:

Give out Student Sheet 8:1.

Read the story out loud with the class. Allow some discussion to clarify any points and emphasise the fact that Josh was in a bad mood when he arrived to meet Millat.

(10 minutes)

Ask students to get into pairs. Ask the pairs to re-read the story together then to think about possible reasons for Josh's bad mood. Get them to draw four line pictures showing these reasons (Student Sheet 8:2).

(Allow 15 minutes)

Bring the whole group together to discuss some of these reasons. Use the board to record some ideas.

(10 minutes)

Use the questions from Teacher Sheet 8:2. Give one question to each pair. Ask them to discuss the question between them, making notes if necessary.

(Allow 10 minutes)

Working as a whole group, ask each pair in turn to say the question and then give their thoughts. Allow plenty of time for discussion. Introduce the term 'empathy' – the ability to see a situation from another person's point of view and feel how they might have felt. Explain that that is what they have been doing. They have been seeing the situation from two points of view: their own and that of the person in the story. Include the following:

- Do they think that if Josh could have felt empathy for Millat after he first yelled at him that would have made a difference?
- Do they think that if Millat had felt empathy for Josh when he first arrived or when he hit him for the second time that things would have been different?

The students can speculate in their discussion about the following things:

- what had happened to Josh before he arrived
- the impact of them being at the big school and not being in the same class all the time
- the role of the friends who separated them
- what they think might happen next
- how being empathic might help both Josh and Millat

(Rest of session)

Josh and Millat were best friends and had been since primary school. They were now both in secondary school and weren't always in the same class anymore. However, they saw a lot of each other and always stayed on after school to kick a football around in the playground.

After school on this particular day, Josh seemed to be distracted and in a bad mood when he arrived. Millat kicked the ball over to him and it accidentally hit Josh in the face. Josh turned round angrily and pushed Millat, yelling at him: "Stupid!!" Millat pushed him back saying: "Hey, that was an accident! Who are you calling stupid?" Josh started to yell some more and hit Millat hard, screaming at him that he had done it on purpose and was trying to make Josh look stupid. Millat retaliated by hitting Josh back harder until they ended up fighting. Fortunately some other friends came up and separated them.

Situation Story

Josh and Millat were best friends and had been since primary school. They were now both in secondary school and weren't always in the same class anymore. However, they saw a lot of each other and always stayed on after school to kick the football around in the playground.

After school on this particular day, Josh seemed to be distracted and in a bad mood when he arrived. Millat kicked the ball over to him and it accidentally hit Josh in the face. Josh turned round angrily and pushed Millat, yelling at him: "Stupid." Millat pushed him back saying, "Hey, that was an accident. Who are you calling stupid?" Josh started to yell some more and hit Millat hard, screaming at him that he had done it on purpose and was trying to make Josh look stupid. Millat retaliated by hitting Josh back harder until they ended up fighting. Fortunately some other friends came up and separated them.

Possible Reasons for Josh's Bad Mood

Scenario 1	Scenario 2
Scenario 3	Scenario 4

Questions About the Story

(photocopy on to card then cut into eight)

What were Josh's feelings when the ball first hit him?	**How could Josh have expressed his feelings when the ball first hit him?**
How do you think Millat felt when he kicked the ball and it hit Josh?	**What do you think Millat was feeling when Josh came at him the second time?**
What do you think Millat could have said or done when Josh came at him for the second time?	**How do you think Millat might have reacted if Josh had been different?**
What do you think Josh could have said or done instead of calling Millat stupid?	**How do you think Millat felt when Josh called him stupid?**

Session 9
Making 'I' Statements

Aims:

To help students learn the steps involved in making 'I' statements.
To compare using 'I' statements with other ways of
communicating.

Resources:

Student Sheet 9:1 'Making 'I' Statements'
Teacher Sheet 9:1 How to Communicate Effectively Using 'I'
Statements

Method:

Tell the students that you are going to do some more work on
anger management and this time you will all be looking at a way to
communicate that helps you repair damage *after* an emotional
hijack, although there are plenty of other situations in which you
can use it too.   Ask the students to think about the two sides to
communication: listening and speaking.   Reinforce the fact that in
Session 6 students practised listening: this time they are going to
be concentrating on the speaking side of the communication.
Emphasise that communicating clearly is very important –
especially if someone isn't listening well.

(5 minutes)

Hand out Student Sheet 9:1 and go over the steps with the class, (Teacher Sheet 9:1 will help you with this).

As you talk through each step, give examples and ask the students to tell you why each step is necessary and important. Ask them to give examples too.

(10 minutes)

Next, you will look at how to make an 'I' statement. The students have this on their worksheet and you will write it on the board prior to this part of the session. Under each step which you have written as a heading begin to work out examples together. Here are some samples, but try to get the students to bring their own ideas too.

"When you ……………………………"

Describe a situation, for example:

- interrupt me so much
- criticise me so much
- tease me about my name
- say things behind my back

"I feel …………………………………"

Statement about how you feel and how the situation is affecting you, for example:

- Frustrated because I want to finish what I am saying
- Angry because I have not always done wrong
- Sad because I like my name
- Hurt because I thought you were my friend
- …………………………………………………..

"And what I want is …………………………………"

Say what you would like to happen instead, for example:

- I'd like you to listen to the end of my story
- Tell me three things that I do that you like
- Not to tease me about my name again
- Stop talking about me when I'm not there
- ……………………………………………….

(Allow 10 minutes)

Now ask students to get into pairs to enact the scenario as explained on Student Sheet 9:1.

(10 minutes)

Ask each pair to join with another to make a group of four and between them to think of another typical situation.

(Allow 5 minutes)

Write the ideas on the board. Working in their groups of four, the students are to work out the 'I' statements for each situation.

(10 minutes)

As a closure activity, hold a general group discussion using the following prompts:

What are some other ways people try to ask for what they want?

- demanding
- whining
- shouting
- criticising

How effective do you think those ways are?

Why is putting what you want into an 'I' statement more effective?

What is the hardest part about the 'I' statements?

How are you going to use this new skill?

When?

(Rest of session)

Making 'I' Statements

Steps

When you want someone to listen to you, you need to send a very clear message. The best way to do that is to follow these steps:

1. ask the person to listen
2. look directly at the listener
3. speak clearly
4. talk in 'I' statements
5. check that the listener has understood
6. thank the listener

Now let's practise these skills. You and your partner are 'A' and 'B' respectively. Take it in turns to be the brother or his friend. Use the following prompts to guide the conversation.

Your brother is playing his music really loudly in the next room and you and your friend are trying to study. You decide to go and talk to him about it. You decide that you will use 'I' statements.

Prompts

"When you ...."

"I feel ...."

"And I'd like you to ...."

How to Communicate Effectively Using 'I' Statements

1. Ask the person to listen – if they are bound up with trying to get their words in, they will not be paying any attention to what you have to say.

2. Look directly at the listener – it is easier for the listener to listen if you keep eye contact. If you look away they think this is a cue for them to speak, or that you have lost interest.

3. Speak clearly – it is hard to listen well if someone is mumbling or shouting incoherently. If you speak clearly it makes it easier for the listener to attend to the content and feelings in what you are saying.

4. Talk in 'I' statements – this takes away the blame in your voice when you say things like 'you are mean' or 'you never do what I want.' You are taking responsibility for yourself and what you want or don't want, and not accusing them.

5. Check that the listener has understood you – it is very easy to misinterpret what someone is saying and asking for a regular 'update' from a listener is a good way to check that they are following your meaning.

6. Thank the listener – they will have worked hard and shown a lot of willingness to be in a relationship with you if they have listened to you like that and they certainly deserve a 'Thank You' for that effort.

Session 10
Rules for Myself

Aims:

To help students make up their own rules for behaviour when they have an emotional hijack.

To evaluate what they have learned about Anger Management.

Resources:

Student Sheet 10:1 Scroll of Rules

Teacher Sheet 10:1 10 Things to do to Control your Anger

Method:

Tell the students that in this session you want them to round up all the learning they have done about Anger Management. Remind them that they have learned:

- how to recognise what they are feeling
- how to name it
- that there are three stages in an emotional hijack
- that emotional hijacks make physical changes in their bodies that they can notice
- that there are many different things they can do during each stage of an emotional hijack

- that they have been practising techniques such as positive self-talk, counting to 10 and using 'I' statements

(5 minutes)

Hand out Student Sheet 10:1 and ask them to get into pairs or fours. Their task is to develop a set of Rules for action to be taken if they experience an emotional hijack in the future. Start them off with some examples from your Teacher Sheet 10.1.

(Allow 15 minutes)

Ask for volunteers to tell you what they have written. Make sure that you praise their suggestions in positive terms. Write the suggestions on the board and discuss any that seem particularly helpful. Ask them to:

- give examples of when they had used that strategy
- say what happened afterwards
- encourage them to talk about triumphs they have had with using something they have just learnt
- use examples when they have seen other people use good techniques

(Allow 15 minutes)

Ask students to find their Learning Log (Student Sheet 1:4) and let them complete it.

(Allow 15 minutes)

Finish the session with a general discussion, asking students to share their ideas with their peers. Some students may wish to share their Learning Logs at this point. Stress that all the techniques they have been learning through the programme are practical ones that will enable them to cope with their feelings of anger more effectively, and that these techniques can be used throughout their lives.

(Rest of session)

Name_____

_____

_____

_____

_____

_____

_____

_____

_____

_____

_____

_____

10 Things to do to Control your Anger

1. Make a list of the things that make you mad and memorise it. Try changing the situations that make you mad.

2. Talk about your feelings. Tell people when things bother you.

3. When you feel really, really angry, sit on your hands and count to 10, breathing very deeply.

4. When you feel so angry that you are about to explode or hit someone, find a physical way to release your energy, such as hitting your pillow, running, or doing push-ups.

5. If you behave badly when you're angry, apologise as soon as possible. It doesn't make things right, but it helps.

6. Instead of getting angry, think about peaceful places like the beach or mountains.

7. Learn to talk to yourself. If you are so angry that you want to scream or hit someone, say to yourself: "Getting angry rarely helps. I can talk things out instead and solve the problem."

8. Be helpful and do good things for people every day. Even if you lose your temper sometimes, people will also remember your good qualities.

9. Set goals for yourself. Think about the kind of person you want to be and work towards becoming that person.

10. Find people who can help you with your anger. There are many adults or friends who will help you when you ask.

Bibliography

Goleman D (1996), *Emotional Intelligence*, Bloomsbury.

Faupel A, Herrick E and Sharp P (1998), *Anger Management*, Fulton Press.

Morris E (1999), *Managing Conflict Calmly*, Buckholdt Press.

Sharp P (2001), *Nurturing Emotional Literacy*, Fulton Press.

The School of Emotional Literacy

The School of Emotional Literacy offers professional training programmes for educators. It provides specialists in emotional intelligence and emotional literacy assessment and development who have become leaders in this field. They provide expert advice and training to schools, LEAs, social services and community education services.

Training and Inset Workshops

The School offers a number of courses related to Self-Esteem and Emotional Literacy and welcomes anyone interested in the development of children, students and young people to their training days and workshops.

Topics include:

- Introducing Emotional Literacy – Release the Potential in your School
- Puppets, Play and Poetry – great methods for developing self-esteem and emotional literacy in pupils
- Emotional Coaching
- The Emotionally Literate Approach to Behaviour Management
- In what ways is that child intelligent? – using Multiple Intelligence Theory in the classroom
- Building Self-Esteem in Children

For the full training list and further information please visit www.schoolofemotional-literacy.com or call 01452 741106.

Incentive Publishing

Incentive Publishing is the publishing division of Incentive Plus, the leading mail-order distributor of topical resources for education.

Visit the Incentive Plus website www.incentiveplus.co.uk to find the UK's largest on-line educational catalogue with hundreds of resources and products for:

- Accelerated Learning
- Anger Management
- Anti-Bullying
- Assertiveness
- Circle Time
- Counselling
- Cultural Diversity
- Drug Education
- Emotional Literacy
- Gifted & Talented
- Life Skills
- Mentoring
- Multiple Intelligences
- Pastoral Care
- Positive Behaviour
- School Councils
- Self-Esteem
- Social Skills
- Special Needs
- Stress Management

To request a free catalogue please contact: Incentive Plus, PO Box 5220, Little Horwood, Milton Keynes MK17 0YN. Telephone: 01908 526120. Fax: 01908 526130. Email: info@incentiveplus.co.uk

THE EMOTIONAL LITERACY APPROACH SERIES

By Elizabeth Morris

Four titles are available in this series:

• Anger Management Programme – Primary
• Anger Management Programme – Secondary
• Assertiveness Programme – Primary
• Assertiveness Programme – Secondary

Each book includes a complete programme of lesson/session plans to use with a class or group. The activities are interactive and fun, and include aims, a list of resources and suggested timings with the outline of the procedure. Teacher notes, pupil/student sheets and handouts are included, the latter of which are all photocopiable.

"This is what I've been waiting for! Anger Management with a directly EL base."
Liz Scott

ORDER FORM

Please send me:

_____ copies of Anger Management: Primary @ £25.00 each

_____ copies of Anger Management: Secondary @ £25.00 each

_____ copies of Assertiveness: Primary @ £25.00 each

_____ copies of Assertiveness: Secondary @ £25.00 each

I enclose a cheque/postal order for £ _____ made payable to Incentive Plus Ltd.

Name_____

Position _____ Establishment_____

Address _____

_____ Postcode_____

Telephone _____ Fax _____

Please post to: Incentive Plus Ltd, PO BOX 5220, Great Horwood, Milton Keynes MK17 0YN, UK.
Telephone: 01908 526120.   Fax: 01908 526130.
Email: orders@incentive.plus.co.uk   www.incentiveplus.co.uk